A gift to -

From -

CROSSOVER! – *transcending cultures for maximum impact*

CROSSOVER!

– transcending cultures for maximum impact

Servant Robin

Published by
SERVANT BOOKS   www.servantministries.co.uk

Distributed by
Robin Jegede-Brimson
Servant Ministries
7, Belton Close, Whitstable, Kent
CT5 4LG, UK
+44(0) 787 202 4364
GodsOyster@aol.com

AFRICA
Henry Hamilton
Servant Ministries Nigeria
U.I.P.O. Box 22974, Ibadan, Nigeria.
+234(0) 80 3368 1552.
hamiltonh78@hotmail.com

Cover design by
BARLT GRAPHICS PRINTS, NIG.
+234(0) 70 3822 8234
topekanbi@yahoo.com

DEDICATION

To my Dad and to my Dad in law,
and to all
in their generation.
Who as young men in their twenties suddenly
found themselves like Daniel in another land,
uprooted and transplanted
from one culture
to another

CROSSOVER! – *transcending cultures for maximum impact*

ACKNOWLEDGEMENTS

F irstly I must thank my father and mother for their courage in a time when inter-racial marriages attracted great opposition and hostility. Thank you for your great bravery born out of your deep love for one another and unconscious knowledge of GOD's will for your lives. Thank you for your wisdom in raising me with a healthy sense of balance between two, often opposing cultures. Together with my wife I am happily poised between the concepts of my home being 'a castle' as well as 'a sanctuary' for all.

For the great gift of my wife, **Nyema** I must also thank her parents, **Prof and Mrs O. A. Nduka** another couple who rode against the times in inter-racial marriage to take their vows, fearing more the loss of their great love than the scorn of those they held dear.

Despite my birthright I still had to choose to learn, rather deliberately how to straddle cultures without giving room for offense to any. For a great season of this experiment I would like to thank the then trio of **Ayodeji Olorunda, Femi Omisade** and **Niyi**

Kolade (of blessed memory) who immersed me quite unexpectedly in the role of founder and pastor of International Church in relatively rural Ibadan, Nigeria. Non-the-less with support from those on the same journey like **Carrie Peters** (an Indian lady) and her daughters **Kim** & **Kelly,** we succeeded in eventually attracting people from more than 40 nations to our services.

I have found that there is a quality that transcends culture with great ease and speaks all languages with great fluency – that of being *kind* and *gracious*. In living memory I can think of non who espouses this quality more than my 'big brother', **Richard Mitchell** being perfectly complimented by his wife **Liz**. Thank you for being perfect models of this quality that inadvertently runs off on others close to you.

Thanks 'Sis', **Monica Jegede** for helping with the section of common grammatical errors.

Lastly in producing this book, I'd like to thank my children **David, Paul, Prince** and **Deborah** as well as my nephew **John** and niece **Sarah,** all who are taking an avid interest in this journey of straddling cultures for the greater good of mankind.

My ever-sweet sweetheart, **Nyema** thank you for the sacrifice and the proofreading.

Thank U* HOLY SPIRIT – U* provide the fuel.

CROSSOVER! – *transcending cultures for maximum impact*

CONTENTS

PREFACE...viii

CHAPTER 1
GOD adores culture..................................1

CHAPTER 2
HIS glory is for the nations......................... 15

CHAPTER 3
Knowing the love of the father.....................27

CHAPTER 4
Love, discipline & manhood........................41

CHAPTER 5
Graced & empowered to integrate..................53

CHAPTER 6
Working Grace Out....................................61

CHAPTER 7
Culturally compatible church settings 89

CROSSOVER! – *transcending cultures for maximum impact*

PREFACE

The 'two-thirds world' church has so much to give. There is no nation on earth, which does not have a deep and key redemptive gifting. I refer to redemptive giftings as areas of grace where a particular group of people have a strong and pronounced area of calling. This gifting is part of the rich spiritual inheritance that ought to be on offer for the rest of The Body of Christ. Just as in understanding spiritual gifts where it is the recipient of the grace that gift brings that is blessed so it is with redemptive giftings; it is only as we tap into and are able to receive that gift that blessing is released.

I remind us of these truths to encourage us. Firstly in the reality of the fact that we are all part of the global body of Christ and have an area of grace that is not meant for us alone but for the wider universal Body of Christ. But more in keeping with the aim of this book we also have a responsibility to make that grace available in cultures other than our own.

What do I mean by this? Simply this – if our forms of communication and our traditions remain encapsulated in the native social setting we are accustomed to, then we alienate those in The Body who need what we have. We have the freely given ministry gifts of Christ and gifts of The HOLY SPIRIT wrapped up in the social culture of our souls. So long as it stays that way, our ministry will be frustrating to us and those we are sent to. We must break the alabaster box of culture to allow the pure fragrance of CHRSIT come out. This is not to destroy the box of culture, not at all, but to necessarily make it subservient to the greater calling of ministry to The LORD, His people and the world.

This is what this book is about.

Enjoy :)

Robin Ayodeji Pierre Jegede-Brimson
Whitstable UK
February 14th 2012

CHAPTER 1

GOD ADORES CULTURE!

CROSSOVER! – *transcending cultures for maximum impact*

"JESUS loves the little children, all the children of
the world,
red and yellow, black and white, they are precious
in his sight; JESUS loves the little children of the
world"

- Traditional Christian children's song

CROSSOVER! – *transcending cultures for maximum impact*

O ur FATHER in heaven loves culture! He loves diversity. The myriads of ethnicities excite our big GOD. Why have one colour when you can have them all? Appears to be His philosophy!

Nowhere is this perhaps as apparent as on the great birthday of the church. The events of this phenomenal day were not by any means left to chance! Creation had waited for this day for thousands of years! The birthing of the body that would liberate the world from darkness, the establishing of a group of common people on whose shoulders the success of the most strategic mission in history would stand. Nothing in this day was allowed to happen by chance. It was all meticulously planned. Particularly the guest list of who would be invited to this party.

Let's look at it in a little detail shall we? The HOLY SPIRIT was about to be poured out on a select group of people. Each placed in this august assembly for a unique purpose.

The grand event- the birthing of the church

And when the day of Pentecost was fully come, they were all with one accord in one place. And suddenly there came a sound from heaven as of a rushing mighty wind, and it filled all the house where they were sitting. And there appeared unto them cloven tongues like as of fire, and it sat upon each of them. And they were all filled with the Holy Ghost, and began to speak with other tongues, as the Spirit gave them utterance. (Acts 2:1-4)

What was the setting?

In the middle of Jerusalem at the time of a major feast, the feast of Pentecost when people from every nation, yes every known people group that could be mustered would come along to attend.

And there were dwelling at Jerusalem Jews, devout men, out of every nation under heaven. Now when this was noised abroad, the multitude came together, and were confounded, because that every man heard them speak in his own language. And they were all amazed and marvelled, saying one to another, Behold, are not all these which speak Galilaeans? And how hear we every man in our own tongue, wherein we were born? Parthians, and Medes, and Elamites, and the dwellers in Mesopotamia, and in Judaea, and Cappadocia, in Pontus, and Asia,

6

Phrygia, and Pamphylia, in Egypt, and in the parts of Libya about Cyrene, and strangers of Rome, Jews and proselytes, Cretes and Arabians, we do hear them speak in our tongues the wonderful works of God. (Acts 2:5-11)

The Effect

It could not have been more powerful! This was something that was totally new; it freaked them all out! 'What's up with these guys?' cried the bewildered crowd. How I would have loved to be able to have seen it all as it unfolded!

And they were all amazed, and were in doubt, saying one to another, What meaneth this? Others mocking said, These men are full of new wine. (Acts 2:12-13)

The Word

Ha ha! From here intrepid Peter launched the offensive, he lost no time in gaining the high ground needed to utilise this great outpouring.

Ye men of Israel, hear these words; Jesus of Nazareth, a man approved of God among you by miracles and

7

wonders and signs, which God did by him in the midst of you, as ye yourselves also know: Him, being delivered by the determinate counsel and foreknowledge of God, ye have taken, and by wicked hands have crucified and slain: Whom God hath raised up, having loosed the pains of death: because it was not possible that he should be holden of it. For David speaketh concerning him, I foresaw the Lord always before my face, for he is on my right hand, that I should not be moved: Therefore did my heart rejoice, and my tongue was glad; moreover also my flesh shall rest in hope: Because thou wilt not leave my soul in hell, neither wilt thou suffer thine Holy One to see *corruption. Thou hast made known to me the ways of life; thou shalt make me full of joy with thy countenance. Men and brethren, let me freely speak unto you of the patriarch David, that he is both dead and buried, and his sepulchre is with us unto this day. Therefore being a prophet, and knowing that God had sworn with an oath to him, that of the fruit of his loins, according to the flesh, he would raise up Christ to sit on his throne; He seeing this before spake of the resurrection of Christ, that his soul was not left in hell, neither his flesh did see corruption. This Jesus hath God raised up, whereof we all are witnesses. Therefore being by the right hand of God exalted, and having received of the Father the promise of the Holy Ghost, he hath shed forth this, which ye now see and hear. For David is not ascended into the heavens: but he saith himself, The Lord said unto my Lord, Sit thou on my right hand, Until I make thy foes thy footstool. Therefore let all the house of Israel know assuredly, that God hath made the same Jesus, whom ye have crucified, both Lord and Christ. (Acts 2:22-36)*

The Fruit

Ahh, the blessing of seeing fruit being swept into the Kingdom of our FATHER! Peter's message in Hebrew together with the exultation and praise of GOD in their own native tongue held the crowd spellbound.

Now when they heard this, they were pricked in their heart, and said unto Peter and to the rest of the apostles, Men and brethren, what shall we do? Then Peter said unto them, Repent, and be baptized every one of you in the name of Jesus Christ for the remission of sins, and ye shall receive the gift of the Holy Ghost. For the promise is unto you, and to your children, and to all that are afar off, even as many as the LORD our God shall call. And with many other words did he testify and exhort, saying, Save yourselves from this untoward generation. Then they that gladly received his word were baptized: and the same day there were added unto them about three thousand souls. (Acts 2:37-41)

The Community

From here the church was birthed - a loving, caring, giving group of people of one heart and one soul.

And they continued steadfastly in the apostles' doctrine and fellowship, and in breaking of bread, and in prayers. And fear came upon every soul: and many wonders and signs were done by the apostles. And all that believed were together, and had all things common; And sold their possessions and goods, and parted them to all men, as every man had need. And they, continuing daily with one accord in the temple, and breaking bread from house to house, did eat their meat with gladness and singleness of heart, Praising God, and having favour with all the people. And the Lord added to the church daily such as should be saved. (Acts 2:42-47)

Years later we have a peek at the feelings and attitudes to race and origin in the early church. We

10

get this snapshot as we read about church in Antioch -

Now there were in the church that was at Antioch certain prophets and teachers; as Barnabas, and Simeon that was called Niger, and Lucius of Cyrene, and Manaen, which had been brought up with Herod the tetrarch, and Saul (Acts 13:1)

They had someone just like me there – (a black guy) as well as a guy from Crete – all captured in the lens of this shot on life in the church at Antioch!

All peoples - The heart and delight of PAPA GOD

GOD loves variety and colour! We have this panoramic view of another celebration that's set for year _ _ _ _? in the calendar of heaven.

And when he had taken the book, the four beasts and four and twenty elders fell down before the Lamb, having every one of them harps, and golden vials full of odours, which are the prayers of saints. And they sung a new song, saying, Thou art worthy to take the book, and to open the seals thereof: for thou wast slain, and hast redeemed us to God by thy blood out of every kindred,

11

and tongue, and people, and nation; And hast made us unto our God kings and priests: and we shall reign on the earth.(Revelation 5:8-10)

The LORD JESUS last will on earth for us

In this well-worn passage our LORD uses a term *ethnae* in the Greek from which we get our English word 'ethnic' Here He was not just talking about political nations but about people groups that comprise those nations. He loves all the tribes.

And Jesus came and spake unto them, saying, All power is given unto me in heaven and in earth. Go ye therefore, and teach all nations, baptizing them in the name of the Father, and of the Son, and of the Holy Ghost: Teaching them to observe all things whatsoever I have commanded you: and, lo, I am with you always, even unto the end of the world. Amen.

What can we do to end suffering and bring peace to our world?

By contributing to one of the vital signs of the imminence of CHRIST's return - taking the good news to as many different peoples as possible.

"But he that shall endure unto the end, the same shall be saved. And this gospel of the kingdom shall be preached in all the world for a witness unto all nations; and then shall the end come" (Matthew 24:12)

Notes . . . .

_____

_____

_____

_____

_____

CHAPTER 2

HIS GLORY IS FOR THE NATIONS!

CROSSOVER! – *transcending cultures for maximum impact*

And I will shake all nations, and the desire of all nations shall come: and I will fill this house with glory, saith the LORD of hosts. (Haggai 2:7)

CROSSOVER! – *transcending cultures for maximum impact*

HEAVENS VIEW OF THE PEOPLES OF THE WORLD

*'In you shall all the families of the nations be blessed'
(Genesis 12:3)*

Right from the time of Abraham, the heart cry of The FATHER has been for the nations. The prophets and the Psalms also continue to reflect this trend. GOD's stated purpose, right from His opening meeting with Abram was that he would make Abram a blessing for the nations of the world. In this we further see GOD's desire for all nations to be blessed.

David, the sweet psalmist of Israel also walked in the consciousness of the same missionary truth – The FATHER's blessing on His people was to serve the added purpose of provoking gentile nations into desiring to know The King!

'God be merciful unto us, and bless us; and cause his face to shine upon us; Selah. That thy way may be known upon earth, thy saving health among all nations. Let the people praise thee, O God; let all the people praise thee. O let the nations be glad and sing for joy: for thou shalt judge the people righteously, and govern the nations

19

upon earth. Selah. Let the people praise thee, O God; let all the people praise thee. Then shall the earth yield her increase; and God, even our own God, shall bless us God shall bless us; and all the ends of the earth shall fear him. '(Psalm 67)

OUR INHERITANCE

One of the great inheritances we can aspire to is to have 'the heathen as our inheritance'.

Ask of me and I will give thee the heathen for your inheritance, the uttermost parts of the world for thy possession.(Psalm 2:8)

But the meek shall inherit the earth; and shall delight themselves in the abundance of peace. (Psalm 37:11)

Repeatedly, David refers to the nations, asking for GOD to visit them, for His light to shine on them, for them to raise their hands to Him.

'Thou hast delivered me from the strivings of the people; and thou hast made me the head of the heathen: a people whom I have not known shall serve me. As soon as they hear of me, they shall obey me: the strangers shall submit themselves unto me'. (Psalm 18:43-44)

20

"For the kingdom is the LORD's: and he is the governor among the nations" (Psalm 22:28)

Neither heaven nor earth will be complete until all the lands clap their hands! He is King over all the earth; we are to be His emissaries to those who are yet to see Him.

'Clap your hands, all ye people; shout unto God with the voice of triumph. For the LORD most high is terrible; he is a great King over all the earth. He shall subdue the people under us, and the nations under our feet. He shall choose our inheritance for us, the excellency of Jacob whom he loved. God is gone up with a shout, the LORD with the sound of a trumpet. Sing praises to God, sing praises: sing praises unto our King, sing praises. For God is the King of all the earth: sing ye praises with understanding. God reigneth over the heathen: God sitteth upon the throne of his holiness' (Psalm 47: 1 – 8)

I will praise thee, O Lord, among the people: I will sing unto thee among the nations. (Psalm 57:9)

Thou therefore, O LORD God of hosts, the God of Israel, awake to visit all the heathen: be not merciful to any wicked transgressors. Selah. (Psalm 59:5)

Make a joyful noise unto God, all ye lands: Sing forth the honour of his name: make his praise glorious. Say unto God, How terrible art thou in thy works! Through the greatness of thy power shall thine enemies submit themselves unto thee. All the earth shall worship thee, and shall sing unto thee; they shall sing to thy name. Selah. Come and see the works of God: he is terrible in his doing toward the children of men. He turned the sea into dry land: they went through the flood on foot: there did we rejoice in him. He ruleth by his power for ever; his eyes behold the nations: let not the rebellious exalt themselves. Selah. Psalm 66

One day, all kings will bow to Him, all over the earth. We are called to proclaim his power and love, so that as they see His power and His goodness they too can be gathered in.

'Yea, all kings shall fall down before him: all nations shall serve him.' (Psalm 72:11)

'All nations whom thou hast made shall come and worship before thee, O Lord; and shall glorify thy name'.(Psalm 86:9)

'Justice and judgment are the habitation of thy throne: mercy and truth shall go before thy face'. (Psalm 89:14)

'Blessed is the people that know the joyful sound: they shall walk, O LORD, in the light of thy countenance.' (Psalm 89:15)

' Say among the heathen that the LORD reigneth: the world also shall be established that it shall not be moved: he shall judge the people righteously'. (Psalm 96:10)

The purpose of the blessing

There is coming a time when the glory of GOD will come mightily upon the church and the nations of the earth will fall at his feet like a pack of cards.

Iris Ministries in Mozambique founded by Rolland & Heidi Baker is just one of such ministries in the world today where a nation has been swept into the kingdom of GOD from a vision to pour out the glory of GOD! This ministry has seen scores of dead raised to life, hundreds of deaf people healed and thousands of orphans being provided for and led into sonship. All this stemmed from a vision for a people who were yet to adequately represented around the throne of GOD. This vision was given in time when The SPIRIT of GOD was visiting a meeting with much glory. Out of it GOD let His heart be known – His longing was for His beloved people!

'Thou shalt arise, and have mercy upon Zion: for the time to favour her, yea, the set time, is come. . . . So the heathen shall fear the name of the LORD, and all the kings of the earth thy glory. When the LORD shall build up Zion, he shall appear in his glory.' (Psalm 102:13-16)

'When the LORD turned again the captivity of Zion, we were like them that dream. Then was our mouth filled with laughter, and our tongue with singing: then said they among the heathen, The LORD hath done great things for them.(Psalm 126:1,2)

The blessing of The LORD on His people is to wake the heathen up - to draw them in.

'And I will shake all nations, and the desire of all nations shall come: and I will fill this house with glory, saith the LORD of hosts.' (Haggai 2:6-8)

'Declare his glory among the heathen; his marvellous works among all nations.' (1 Chronicles 16:23-25)

Notes . . . .

_____

_____

_____

_____

_____

CROSSOVER! – *transcending cultures for maximum impact*

CHAPTER 3

TRANSFORMED
BY THE LOVE OF
THE FATHER

CROSSOVER! – *transcending cultures for maximum impact*

"Behold what manner of love the FATHER has given unto us . . . " (1John 3:1)

CROSSOVER! – *transcending cultures for maximum impact*

The love of The FATHER frees us from a performance mentality. It liberates us from a mindset that depends on ones own ability to pray, to fast, and to tithe. It frees from a perspective that it is only when I do those things that I am in favour and in right standing with my father.

No, GOD loves you just as you are. You are a delight to Him, warts and all! Just like a father dotes on his 2-week-old baby before the child has had an opportunity to earn that love – you cannot earn the love of GOD, only receive it and walk in it. You are loved, your dad googles and drools over you. He is delightedly pleased with you!

The statement 'My beloved son in whom I am well pleased' came before our LORD did any miracle, or fasted or withstood the temptations of the evil one. He was already loved and secure in that love. It was from this position that He was released to go into the wilderness and to ultimately face the enemy. He was never in doubt that it was not about earning fathers love. That was already settled.

Love from PAPA-GOD was given at the starting blocks; it was the starting point of his ministry. It was not withheld on a 'Lets wait and see' perspective. So it couldn't ever be earned. JESUS went out and did His stuff because He knew who He was. He got His identity sorted prior to warfare. So when the enemy came with, *'If you are the son of . . .'*, hey mister, that question has already been resolved, there's no issue on that score!

Now, as you receive this love it will change your perspectives of who you are. This always leads to tremendous liberty and freedom, free from a need for titles, accolades and clamouring for position. Like a bird set free from a cage you fly, like a kite let loose in the park on a windy day, you soar! Why? You know who you are in Christ, secure in PAPA's love and embrace. Ha Ha!

PROPHETIC WORD

"For I long for you to walk in your true identity as sons before Me, it is only with this freedom that you will be able to enter My rest, My inner courts and curl up with Me knowing Me as FATHER. Free to enter my refrigerator and raid my larder; to come up with the most outrageous and absurd demands because you are my child! Free to ask for anything! Free to forgive yourself as Peter did and as David did. Free from accusations from the enemy, their words will be like water off a ducks back as an invisible film of love and my approval shields you.

Know my love, step into my courts and chambers. I love you and delight for you to step into my innermost chambers beyond the outer courts and abide in intimacy with me. I love you. The prayer of Jesus was that I would love you as I loved Him, my first begotten Son and I have answered that prayer, that longing of His soul for Me to love and accept you because of what He did at Calvary. And I have added favour to that love. Come into the innermost chambers, the veil has been torn down and stripped away for you to have access and gain entry and come on in. Why do you gaze at the past and see yourself dirty in filthy garments? Remove them. Be dressed in the finest of livery. I have called you. I have loved you and robed you in white garments and kingly robes, bedecked you in gold that you may abide with me and always be my 'favourite child' and play and abide in My courts. So come as you are with the name I have given you and loved you with, 'My beloved' 'My chosen one' 'The one in whom My soul delights'. You need no other name or title from men when you are secure in Me, your loving father. You are My beloved, My delight. My favoured one. I have loved you and chosen you from all the people of the earth. Abide in My love, let nothing take this away or rob you of it. Your sins are washed away, to be remembered no more. I have taken away your reproach, I rebuke kings for your sake and given men in exchange for you, you are My delight, whoever touches you touches the apple of my eye. I give all for you my child. Rest and abide in my love 24-7. Never do anything out of anything, or for any other reason than My love for you, being compelled by My love. Let My love be your fuel, your fire, your zeal, your energy, your motivation, whatever is not done from My love is not done for Me and it will not bear lasting fruit. On that day it will be burnt up and its fruit will perish. For I am building a kingdom based on My love, My empire will be built on love. Fleshly works will not prevail.

As you love Me and I give you My heart and compassion and My power. Let your heart swell with My love, let it full your life, every waking moment, your thoughts, your motive your doings be compelled by My love let it take you across the road, across the streets, across the places of darkness, into the brothels, the gambling halls, the high ways and byways where the poor the destitute are, to wherever people are seeking for truth and for Me, into the prisons, the hospitals, to a people you have never seen.

Let it move you to a nation and as you pour that love into a community and society, into a nation, it will be a funnel of liquid gold being poured out. New green grass will grow, new plants will spring up, new trees, oaks of righteousness will spring up, old river beds will flow again, gold fish will be found in them and lilies will sprout up. My sun will shine in places of dreariness; the fog will go as my rain and love shine down.

In place of disjointed broken families will come dads no longer separated from sons. I will restore harmony. The young will marry and cohabit in peace, they will be faithful to one another, and the children will grow in safety and security. Homes will stand with homes and they will take on the widows, the forsaken, the oppressed. Social care will flow from My community once again and I will fill My house with glory again says The LORD. But I have caused you and called you to first be filled with My love. So come to Me each of you not as adults not as achievers or leaders or people of worth nor stature but come as little babes, strip away your titles and come as I created you, given a name by their parents, and I will receive you, nurture you and release you to your identity as kings and priests, I will groom and release you in the house of love that you may bear My name and likeness to your community and to the nations I call you to go to.

Fear not, fear will be far from you. And oppression from you, you will be perfected in my love. Sickness, disease and darts and bullets of the enemy will stop short of you, because you will be operating in the most powerful force in all of creation – the power of love, My love. For many even their physical appearance will change as they come close to you, forces of life and creation itself will change, the grass and greenery of the trees; flowers and fields will be impacted as they recognise My spirit upon and within you, yea there will be miracles of physical re-birth, mighty acts in creation stemming from My love oozing from the atmosphere around you permeating saturated by My love ,

So walk in love, be grounded in love, rooted in love, speak the truth I love, grow in love, be edified in love, perfected in loved, come together in loved. For I have much to accomplish, many hearts to reach and touch and ultimately transform not by programs and laudable events but by the hot liquid gold of divine love flowing from heaven to earth through you, My sons and servants.

A warm flow of evidenced of grace bubbles up in you, sprouting out as I redig the wells of compassion in you. I will renew and refill and expand your hearts for a mighty gushing and spewing forth of my love on the planet. It will be an avalanche of love.

The most wicked places on earth will be touched and reached like never before. Fear not, many will be martyred out of love even as Stephen was and it will spark a revival of love and compassion as scores more go to take their places. In the many nations the fortes of extremism and religious hatred will be quenched and extinguished as waves and blankets of My love come on earth swarming their communities. Fear not for your life is held in My hands

I will use you, learn and be prepared to not love you life even unto death to go to the darkest places in your planet, some are right next to you at your door step and your armoury will be My love.

Fear not my love is greater and will be over you as a cloud, I have loved you. Many waters cannot quench love"

Notes . . . .

CROSSOVER! – *transcending cultures for maximum impact*

CHAPTER 4

LOVE, DISCIPLINE & MANHOOD

CROSSOVER! – *transcending cultures for maximum impact*

And ye have forgotten the exhortation which speaketh unto you as unto children, My son, despise not thou the chastening of the Lord, nor faint when thou art rebuked of him: For whom the Lord loveth he chasteneth, and scourgeth every son whom he receiveth. If ye endure chastening, God dealeth with you as with sons; for what son is he whom the father chasteneth not? But if ye be without chastisement, whereof all are partakers, then are ye bastards, and not sons. Furthermore we have had fathers of our flesh which corrected us, and we gave them reverence: shall we not much rather be in subjection unto the Father of spirits, and live?For they verily for a few days chastened us after their own pleasure; but he for our profit, that we might be partakers of his holiness. Now no chastening for the present seemeth to be joyous, but grievous: nevertheless afterward it yieldeth the peaceable fruit of righteousness unto them which are exercised thereby. Wherefore lift up the hands which hang down, and the feeble knees; And make straight paths for your feet, lest that which is lame be turned out of the way; but let it rather be healed.
(Hebrews 12:5-13)

OVERCOMING INERTIA AS WE EXPERIENCE
FATHERS LOVE

For there is no difference between the Jew and the Greek:
for the same Lord over all is rich unto all that call upon
him. For whosoever shall call upon the name of the Lord
shall be saved. How then shall they call on him in whom
they have not believed? And how shall they believe in
him of whom they have not heard? And how shall they
hear without a preacher? And how shall they preach,
except they be sent? as it is written, How beautiful are
the feet of them that preach the gospel of peace, and bring
glad tidings of good things (Romans 10:12-15)

N o difference at all Paul pleads between them
and us! We are all the same colour under our
skins! Now get up and go he pleads!
Historically even in Paul's time often there would
need to be another push to get them going. Even
GOD's best sheep can sometimes be reluctant to
move out beyond their comfort zone. Yes, to be fair
we do have great examples like Paul and Silas who
received a very clear and accompanying grace to
take the gospel to other peoples. But we also see
how Jonah needed to be persuaded should we say,
to go on GOD's mission to those 'hostile foreigners'.
Let's face it, it isn't always easy and doesn't always

come naturally. Racism, prejudice and intolerance are all natural tendencies in humans. It can be born out of different reasons, sometimes it is fear of the unknown. Why do they talk that way? Why are they so loud? Or so quiet? How do they manage to eat THAT! On and on the list goes. How do we break free from this culture of bigotry? By the love of GOD. By receiving The FATHER'S love firstly for ourselves then for the peoples of the world He has called us to love and serve.

Over and over again as the glory of GOD is mentioned as coming onto the earth it is connected with the nations – the various peoples of the earth. His Glory wants to flow through you. His power wants to be revealed at a level and dimension you've never known. But His question is, 'Will you take it to the nations? Or keep it to yourself?

LOVE AND DISCIPLINE GO HAND IN HAND

Back to our discourse on overcoming inertia. Often the case is that events take place to push us out of our nests and into the harvest fields. In Jerusalem in the 1st century it took a mighty persecution to get the message across to the church. The result?

And at that time there was a great persecution against the church which was at Jerusalem; and they were all scattered abroad throughout the regions of Judaea and Samaria (Acts 8:1)

They needed this 'special medicine' to fulfil the great commission. GOD could not leave them alone to the realm of being 'led by The SPIRIT of GOD' to go. This was not a case of 'I am feeling led', or 'Let me first go and pray about it' it was, 'You will go by force!' like it or not.

As for Saul, he made havock of the church, entering into every house, and haling men and women committed them to prison. Therefore they that were scattered abroad went everywhere preaching the word.

I tell you, to know GOD's love is also to know His chastisement. They go together.

And ye have forgotten the exhortation which speaketh unto you as unto children, My son, despise not thou the chastening of the Lord, nor faint when thou art rebuked of him: For whom the Lord loveth he chasteneth , and

47

scourgeth every son whom he receiveth . If ye endure chastening, God dealeth with you as with sons; for what son is he whom the father chasteneth not? But if ye be without chastisement, whereof all are partakers, then are ye bastards, and not sons. Furthermore we have had fathers of our flesh which corrected us, and we gave them reverence : shall we not much rather be in subjection unto the Father of spirits, and live ? (Hebrews 12:6-9)

Even the great man of GOD, Phillip the deacon who stood next to Stephen the first martyr (from Acts chapter 6-7) could not be trusted to first 'see a vision' of the needy people in Samaria. We are not always as spiritual as we think ourselves to be. He was thrust out!

Then Philip went down to the city of Samaria, and preached Christ unto them. And the people with one accord gave heed unto those things which Philip spake , hearing and seeing the miracles which he did . . . And there was great joy in that city.

There was great joy in the city, yes, but there needed to first be some pain on the part of the people who would go before joy could be released.

SUPREME MODE OF DIVINE GUIDANCE

So, here is my point – what pain have you had to
endure in coming from whatever nation your
forefather's originated from to this nation you are
now in? What have been the extraneous
circumstance that forced your hand? Or that of your
parent's hands? It is not in vain. May it not go to
waste. May the plan and purpose of GOD in brining
you to where you are come to pass.

It is GOD who ultimately determined that you are
where you are now. It is the supreme mode of
divine guidance – circumstance. Like I said earlier,
whether you are 'led' or 'not led' – you can never
argue with the voice of circumstance that has
determined where you are now.

*God that made the world and all things therein, seeing
that he is Lord of heaven and earth, dwelleth not in
temples made with hands; Neither is worshipped with
men's hands, as though he needed any thing, seeing he
giveth to all life, and breath, and all things; And hath
made of one blood all nations of men for to dwell on all
the face of the earth, and hath determined the times before
appointed , and the bounds of their habitation; That they*

49

should seek the Lord, if haply they might feel after him,
and find him (Acts 17:24-26)

So, you are here now. And you are faced with three
options – make another Goshen for yourself while
you stay in this Egypt. Keep to yourself and let
GOD bless you 'in your small corner and I in mine'
as it goes. Or you can hang up your harps and
weep, "How can we sing the LORD's song in a
strange land?' (Psalm 137:4) or there is a third way.
'Your people will be my people and your GOD will
be my GOD' it was to this courage woman that
David the man after GOD's heart was born. What if
she held back like Orpah and refused to integrate?
What a loss to the world and to her too. Do not lose
all FATHER brought you to this strange land that
you are in to achieve.

Notes . . . .

CROSSOVER! – *transcending cultures for maximum impact*

CHAPTER 5

GRACED &
EMPOWERED TO
INTEGRATE

CROSSOVER! – *transcending cultures for maximum impact*

.

But ye shall receive power, after that the Holy Ghost is come upon you: and ye shall be witnesses unto me both in Jerusalem, and in all Judaea, and in Samaria, and unto the uttermost part of the earth. (Acts 1:8)

'Then he answered and spake unto me, saying , This is the word of the LORD unto Zerubbabel, saying , Not by might, nor by power, but by my spirit, saith the LORD of hosts. Who art thou, O great mountain? before Zerubbabel thou shalt become a plain: and he shall bring forth the headstone thereof with shoutings, crying, Grace, grace unto it. Moreover the word of the LORD came unto me, saying, The hands of Zerubbabel have laid the foundation of this house; his hands shall also finish it; and thou shalt know that the LORD of hosts hath sent me unto you. For who hath despised the day of small things?' (Zechariah 4:6-10)

You are not alone, GOD your maker, The ONE who created you with a desire for the foods you eat and the clothes you wear and the jokes you like is with you on this mission. He is very near. Do not be intimidated by the giants in the land or the obstacles you face. With GOD's help they will become a plain. Your start may be start, but with His help you can grow and multiply. Key to this is lining up with your purpose.

As Paul identified his purpose in GOD for seeing The LORD, he was able to ask for and receive grace to communicate the gospel to the gentile nations. To make all men 'see the fellowship of the mystery of Christ'

Whereof I was made a minister, according to the gift of the grace of God given unto me by the effectual working of his power. Unto me, who am less than the least of all saints, is this grace given, that I should preach among the Gentiles the unsearchable riches of Christ; And to make all men see what is the fellowship of the mystery. (Ephesians 3:7-8)

Coming out of our shells and semi-spiritual and semi-cultural enclaves to open up to the societies we find ourselves in is part of identifying our purpose. This process is both a work of The SPIRIT, as well as a work of our minds and souls. It is a spiritual journey fuelled by the call of GOD, every call is apportioned a level of grace. Now, we may not all end up like Sunday Adelaja, a Nigerian who pastors Europe's largest church with over 10,000 people in the Ukraine, but must go look beyond our call and press into an understanding of that grace gift that is attached to it.

"Work out your salvation with fear and trembling . . .GOD is at work in you both to will and to do of His good pleasure" (Philippians 2:12-13)

The LORD asked the apostles and the 120 who gathered together in the upper room to wait for an empowerment to communicate the gospel to all nations. That empowering included grace to communicate the love and beauty of GOD in languages they never learnt to peoples from different cultures. That grace was given to us at Pentecost, it us ours on coming to CHRSIT and experiencing His indwelling power.

But he giveth more grace. Wherefore he saith, God resisteth the proud, but giveth grace unto the humble.So, what are the keys to this treasure of grace? (James 4:6)

Walking in hunger, walking in humility, walking in openness to revelation.

Notes . . . .

_____

_____

_____

_____

_____

CHAPTER 6

WORKING
GRACE OUT

CROSSOVER! – *transcending cultures for maximum impact*

Even so faith, if it hath not works, is dead, being alone.
Yea, a man may say, Thou hast faith, and I have works:
shew me thy faith without thy works, and I will shew
thee my faith by my works.
(James 2:17-18)

CROSSOVER! – *transcending cultures for maximum impact*

The former treatise have I made, O Theophilus, of all that
Jesus began both to do and teach (Acts 1:1)

Learning requires both teaching as well as doing. It is as we put into practise all our minds and hearts assimilate that we go through the crossover and begin to absorb new ways of doing things.

This chapter is about key areas where we need to make those transitions to become better ambassadors of Christ in varying cultural settings.

Zeroing in on an African / West European cultural mix

There are hundreds if not thousands of cultural combinations that we may all be coming from and seeking to integrate to. Right now there are Philipino believers seeking to save the lost in Saudi Arabia, Chinese workers in Yemen and Brazilians in Uganda. The principles remain the same whatever the culture you are trying to reach. In his list of languages on face book a friend included 'American English' in his list of languages!

Most of what we will look at in this chapter has to do with people from a basic African background integrating with a generally western culture.

Wherever we are from there are 6 basic areas we need to do our homework in.

1. Language & Phonetics
2. Etiquette & Taboo's
3. Food & Drink
4. Fun & Recreation
5. Land & Geography
6. Dress & Appearance

1. LANGUAGE & PHONETICS.

'If the bugle gives an indistinct sound how will the people prepare for battle?' *(1Corinthians 14:9)* still holds true today. Many people in the setting in which the New Testament was written were fluent in Hebrew, Greek and Aramaic. The ruling class across Europe in the most of the last few centuries all could communicate verbally as well as culturally in the major European languages. I say culturally as well because culture goes along with language. I cannot greet my father meaningfully in Yoruba (our native tongue) and adopt an English posture. Part of the school curricula in my father's day was to learn Latin and today children in the west learn Spanish, French and German. The Korean pastor of the largest church in the world, Paul Yonggi-Cho is still learning languages and has added Japanese to his list. Why? A burning desire to go beyond the borders of culture to impact another people. Why not you? Why not me?

Two areas to constantly improve on are our vocabulary and our diction. It is not enough, to excuse poor performance by lamely saying, 'It is not my mother tongue', this is not an excuse. In a culture of excellence (propounded in true

67

Charismatic church tradition) we want to do everything as right as right can be. *'Whatever your hand finds to do, do with all your might'* *(Ecclesiastes 9:10)*

Let's keep working on both areas. Have a person (or persons) who you are open to for them to come to you after your sermon (I have someone who does it in the middle of mine!) to point out that embarrassing gaff or blunder. It keeps us preachers humble and approachable.

As a start here is a list of common grammatical English mistakes: -

1. 'Themselves' when referring to 'each other'
2. 'Reverse back' – could one reverse forwards?
3. Using the incorrect genders with pronouns; using 'he' and 'she' almost interchangeably in conversations.
4. Difficulty in pronouncing 'th', so, 'anyting'. Three pronounced as 'tree' etc
5. No and yes for many African's do not have the required, -*thank you* and -*please* added on. It's not rude just cultural, but viewed as quite rude to the English.

6. In answer to the question 'Where's your manager?' the African often will respond with, 'not on seat' or 'not around'. It sounds posh to an African ear but weird to a European ear.

7. In churches asking people to sit down, an African way of putting it is often, 'Have your seat' rather than, 'You may be seated' or 'Please do sit down'

8. The word 'sorry' is used by an African to show empathy and sympathy for any unfortunate occurrence. This covers all from tripping on the pavement to loss of a dear one. This sounds strange to a westerner where sorry has a connation of apologising/being at personal fault for something.

9. When asked to comment on a piece of work an appropriate response from an African would be, 'You are trying' meaning, well done, great job, keep it up! not quite the same to English ears.

10. 'Tea' to an African means any form of beverage, so hot chocolate could be referred to as 'cocoa tea' etc

11. 'Welcome' and 'well done' are used as universal greetings in an African setting. A little more than in a western one.

Can we think of some more where mistakes are often made? I still fall for the 'sorry' one!

Does it matter you say? For many reasons, Yes!

- Different words mean different things. I have been around westerners who misunderstood totally what was being said! For example an otherwise thrilling testimony of some ones 'goose' being recovered referring to their 'goods'!

- Some words mean nothing at all to the westerners ears if to far from the norm.

- Wrongly pronounced words can be a put off. Benny Hinn and other ministers like him take great pains to perfectly orchestrate a service to take the peoples eyes of themselves and into GOD's Healing Presence. It would be a bad place when half way into GOD's presence to land a clanger!

70

We all get better with practise. Let's make it one of life's journeys.

Notes . . . .

_____

_____

_____

_____

_____

2. TABOO'S & ETIQUETTE

MEAL TIMES

How different cultures can be – approach a typical African during meal times and he will immediately assume you must join him for food, to refuse may cause offence. For a westerner they will assume you are going to excuse yourself (apologise for coming during mealtime) and so will expect you to wait in another room while they finish their meal. Two different ways of handling things. We need to be comfortable with both while seeking a biblical tradition within our culture.

TIMING

Approaches to punctuality and time keeping are very different in western and African cultures. The westerner has an innate ability to make allowances for last minute domestic issues, judge traffic conditions and remember to make room to stop for that last minute item at the shops all in time for that 5pm appointment! 'That 5pm' to an African however often translates to, 'At 5pm I need to remember that I am meant to be somewhere and begin to make a conscious effort to pause what else I am doing and begin to move towards that direction' 5pm is like the town crier, get reasdy to come to the square! There is little demand to actually be there at 5pm – that would be pointless, no one is actually expected to be there at 5pm! 5pm is merely the target time.

In a western setting for any meeting, people are conditioned to gather BEFORE 5pm, so that the meeting actually starts at 5pm. In coming to live in England I found this confusing and after a while embarrassing!

From an African perspective, it is perfectly OK to 'begin to gather at shortly after 5pm' – 'as soon as we feel enough people are around we will start the meeting'

This is not in any way to disparage one system in preference of another. No way. Both systems work perfectly well in their individual social contexts; we only have a problem when we try to mix both cultures together. I for one, am often unstuck when invited to a meeting if I do not accurately judge the social context of the meeting I am about to attend. I get it wrong sometimes by arriving at such an early hour (western punctuality?) as to embarrass my guests! They would much rather I strolled in an hour or so after the advertised time to give people time to 'settle down'. Much less pressure. (It goes without saying how this acts in reverse when a westerner is invited to an appointment)

Which time system are we functioning in? We need to make up our minds and be clear. Then be unapologetic about our decisions.

P's & Q's

In certain African cultures thanks are offered days after a good deed is done. So on meeting that particular person even a few days or a week after an event it is normal to refer to the good deed done and thank the person again, and again, and again . .

Westerners are not like this, they feel that to overemphasise or be 'over grateful' to a good deed might risk oneself becoming 'beholden' to that person. Westerners value their independence.

However the westerner does take very seriously the protocol of daily 'please' and 'thank you'. This is nothing to do with hierarchy and the same niceties are required of boss or servant alike. Good breeding demands it of all westerners, a failure in this area will very quickly betray love and trust.

CULTURAL TURN OFFS

Sweat is normal to an African. We cannot do without it. We sweat as we toil in the farms, we sweat as we play on the fields, we sweat as we eat that peppery stew, and we sweat as we dance before The LORD. It is normal.

Why would the European pay so much attention to having odourless armpits? Yet they do. They also go to great lengths to keep odour killing chewing gum at hand at all times, lest people are slain with 'dragons breadth!' While on this topic people of both cultures can be very guilty of not changing clothes daily just because they do not seem dirty. A nicety easy to neglect in the cold western hemisphere.

Notes . . . .

_____

_____

_____

_____

_____

3. FOOD & DRINK

Food, 'the way to a mans heart' but served properly! Someone close to me was entertaining a potential suitor with a lovingly prepared portion of sausage and chips; but alas the ketchup was forgotten!

We all love the foods we grew up on, in just a few years from birth by the time we reach our early teens so much of our palate is set. We sometime we need to unset it! There is a whole world of food out there these days – English traditional roasts to start with if we are called to the UK, then there's Italian pizza's and lasagne, the range of Indian curries, Chinese buffets and Mexican cheeses. It's a great way to integrate with other cultures.

Drink. I have no problem with people who drink or who don't. What is a problem is people who are dogmatic in their position on this. Especially if the bible is used to try to justify a position. Interacting with Christians the world over leads to an obvious conclusion - Drink is a sub-Christian cultural issue. Once we recognise it as a cultural stance it is easier to adapt as necessary in integrating with the culture we are seeking to reach.

Notes . . . .

_____

_____

_____

_____

_____

4. FUN & RECREATION

In trying to reach our set group of people all information about their popular culture is invaluable in building bridges and pulling down barriers. Questions we might need to ask are: -

- What makes for a fun outing in the culture of those we are trying to reach? Walking the dog? Playing monopoly with the kids? Going for a swim? Seeing the new block buster at the cinema?

- Where do the ladies meet up? In the supermarket? While preparing a meal?

- Where do the men relax? In the Pub? At the gym? Watching football?

- What is comedy to them? Why do they find that so funny?

- What TV soaps are popular?

- Who are their national heroes? Tennis players? Movie stars? Members of their royal family?

81

- What is their national sport? Football? Rugby? Darts?

- What are safe conversational topics? Politics? The weather? Football? The economy? What's not safe? Beware!

Notes . . . .

_____

_____

_____

_____

_____

5. LAND & GEOGRAPHY

On starting ministry in the England back in 2002, for the first several months we would always sing the national anthem and pray for the Queen and royal family. It seems a strange thing to do when I look back at it now. This was my part of saying I wanted to honour what mattered to the UK, I desired to integrate with my new adopted homeland.

The search to learn more about England, Scotland, Wales and Ireland is an ever-continuous one. This search includes learning about the geography of this new place. Certain things like the pronunciation of places like Grosvenor House, Edinburgh and Edgeware Road are less mysterious as we expose ourselves to the places around.

I find it helpful to 'enlist' friends who can act as my local 'culture guides' - friends who will tell me about my area of the country.

Notes . . . .

6. DRESS & APPEARANCES

I recall the attention I gave to the shape of my tie in my first few sermons in England. Oh, my suit mattered so much to me then. One successful missionary European church planter quips, 'You print handbills with your picture on the front and hand them out, yet the people you are trying to reach are too busy walking their dogs to come and see a man dressed up in a suit!' With the possible exceptions of certain churches in America we need to ask if suits are still in vogue as 'Sunday best'?

I like the way Paul Jinadu, founder of the worldwide 'New Covenant Church' stream puts it, 'Why make dress codes which are barriers to people you are trying to reach getting inside your church building?' 'Some churches are the only places in the world where people are asked to sit an exam (about dress codes) before they are even taught' 'It is not the outside we want to change but the inside which will ultimately reflect on the outside'

Visiting two churches near my hometown in Nigeria, in one church everyone is wearing a suit with the ladies all wearing hats – looking like people from 19th century Europe. In the other church people dress naturally and normally, they wear everyday clothes and are not coerced into wearing some form of unofficial uniform. Which do we think is a better model?

Let's free people to come as they are- smart, casual, garden clothes, let's pull down the barriers.

Notes . . . .

_____

_____

_____

_____

_____

CHAPTER 7

CULTURALLY COMPATIBLE CHURCH SETTINGS

Make a joyful noise unto God, all ye lands
(Psalm 66:1)

Coming from a background that is foreign to a new culture there are two barriers to church attendance to be aware of – a social one and a spiritual one.

The social one is obvious – this could be evident in having things like a different skin colour, a thick accent, a foreign dress style, a different timing ethic etc. we need to be aware that these cultural differences exist and do our best to minimise if not eliminate most of them.

The other area is our ethic expression of spirituality. How we do church. For an African seeking to reach a westerner there are three areas to watch out for in this: -

1. **A strong emphasis on tongues and spiritual warfare.** I am all for tongues and warfare in the spirit but the question we need to ask is, 'Am I being wise in my choice of time and place for it?' Half an hour on a Sunday morning at the start of the service may, or may not be the best setting. Paul's admonition as to what an unbeliever in any society will make of this should keep us in

check. (See 1Corinthians 14:23). I remember several years ago being approached by a faithful member of my church, she had a friend who was curious and wanted to explore Christianity. The only problem was, when would be a good time for my church member to bring her friend to a meeting? In other words, without a risk of her being scared off? All our meetings both Sundays and mid week were so spiritual that we had no meeting she felt confident enough about to bring her enquiring friend to!

Beware also an over-emphasis on warfare as a panacea to social evil. Not all problems are solved by prayer; some need compassionate social action.

2. **An emphasis on material prosperity and fulfilling personal destiny**. These messages are required more by people who are in the early stages of settling into a new culture and faced with new economic challenges and choices. It is interesting to me in my travels to see the different ethnic representations in health and prosperity

meetings, or revival meetings etc. All cultures require different messages to appeal to their worldviews. As well as to scratch where they are itching, otherwise a scratch where there is no itch proves to be irritating rather than soothing.

3. **A penchant for personal titles and positions.** Too much emphasis on designations can be a turn off to people new to a church. Titles and a strict adherence to them do two things – they build barriers (not bridges), they unduly place those have these titles on a plane above the rest of the congregation. (Good to receive from them, not good to empower and liberate them) If at all titles are used it is best to keep them simple and informal. It can also be wisdom to let a title follow our good deeds rather than precede them. It is vastly more important to function in an office than to have a title to that office.

SUNDAY SERVICES

We need to ask ourselves the question, do we want our services to be 'seeker friendly' or like an intensive boot camp / swot team? Or somewhere in between? A great way to solve the need for both is to have a morning meeting, which is more suited to the enquirer and perhaps an alternative meeting (in the evening?) designed for the more mature committed believer.

SMALL GROUP MEETINGS

This is a whole topic by itself but here are the leading questions we need to ask in seeking for wisdom in transcending cultural issues. Is the vision for the small group: -

> a. To be a 'nurture group' for the converted or one that seeks to interface with the surrounding community?

b. To grow and develop the gifting of the host/primary leader or the group as a whole?

c. To develop into an independent church standing on it's own? Or to multiply into new small groups?

d. To attract growth from the main church or from the neighbourhood?

Depending on our answers to these questions we may need to apply: -

a. Fun and creativity in our use of jokes, stories and icebreakers.

Or

b. Principles to align with 1Corinthians 14:26 'each one has a tongue, a revelation'

Whichever route we decide to take I would like to encourage a healthy dose of two ingredients – **hospitality** and ample does of **social interaction**. Both of these are thoroughly biblical. The church in Acts met 'from house to house', they were involved in healthy community relationships. This is how they arrived at having 'favour with all the people'. Being social is by no means an anti-thesis to being spiritual.

Hospitality is listed several times in the scriptures as a key entry point to the operation of spiritual gifts. To be genuinely hospitable requires one to first have heartfelt love, empathy and concern; the bedrock for the gifts as described by Paul in 1Corinthians 13.

"Having then gifts differing according to the grace that is given to us, whether prophecy, let us prophesy according to the proportion of faith; Or ministry, let us wait on our ministering: or he that teacheth, on teaching; Or he that exhorteth, on exhortation: he that giveth, let him do it with simplicity; he that ruleth, with diligence; he that sheweth mercy, with cheerfulness. Let love be without dissimulation . . . instant in prayers; **given to hospitality"** *(Romans 12:6-13)*

" **Use hospitality** *one to another without grudging. As every man hath received the gift, even so minister the same one to another, as good stewards of the manifold grace of God. If any man speak, let him speak as the oracles of God; if any man minister, let him do it as of the ability which God giveth" (1Peter 4:9-11)*

98

EVANGELISTIC METHODS

Two issues here –

A) Do you desire to pursue a model of evangelism as an event that the church from time to time partakes in? or an every everyday expected lifestyle for every believer?

B) What evangelistic methods will work and what will be a turn off I your particular societal context?

Statistically by far the most new people are added through your existing members; those already with you are your best ministry ads. As they grow in maturity and obedience to the prompts of that inner voice they will grow your church.

It can be great to mobilise our people into 'soul winning' outings. But in doing so there is an excess we need to be on the look out for – a mindset that focuses primarily on discharging our responsibility in getting the message out and not on the people receiving it. It goes something like this – 'I don't want 'blood guilt' (for not telling the sinner about JESUS) on my hands so I will tell them. If as a result of the way I tell them about JESUS they never talk to me again then I am not too bothered, at least I have fulfilled my 'responsibility' in 'warning them'.

Standing on the street corner distributing tracts might not be the most effective evangelistic model in 21st century western society. To the zealous soul winner - it is not about you assuaging your conscience that you have gone out to proclaim the truth. We have a higher responsibility to love than to proselytise.

There are various evangelistic tools that are culturally relevant to western society. The Alpha Course, Prophetic Evangelism, Healing evangelism and Fun Days etc.

CHECK LIST

Making rules for uncompromising growth and integration

Care for the weak
If your church is predominantly non-indigenous European – maintain an evening service for the ethnic minority in the congregation. (Freeing yourself to make changes in the morning one) Certain people need the comfort of being with their own people – psychologically. Without this time together they will resent the intrusion of 'foreigners' into their home space, which is the only time, and comfort they have – they are missing home!

Staff your weaknesses
Compensate for your area of weakness. If your accent is thickly African fall in love with cricket. If you love western food celebrate it and use it in hospitality

Keep your identity
Personally I do not encourage name changes, a popular form of this is using your Christian name rather then your more popular indigenous name. Names have to do with identity, we are not talking

about abandoning ones own culture but about being able to conform to another culture in it's own distinct setting. Becoming multi cultural.

Food and drink

This is a key area. Shift to the predominant drink and snack of the culture you are trying to reach out to.

Language

It goes without saying that in the setting of your 'normal' service only your host nations language should be heard.

Playing their tune

Observe that the music style of your host culture- is it led by guitars or keyboards? What is the level of the drumming content? A key area to keep tabs on it seeking to draw in people from another culture is that of the music. Bend over backwards to incorporate as many people from that grouping as possible into your worship team. So that they are visible? No. because, there style will almost always be quite different to yours.

Sermons

Speak to the people you want to attract. Even if they are not there yet, you control who is coming and who is staying by your ministry emphasis – the right ones will come in!

PERSONAL NOTES
Notes . . . .

A prayer to receive JESUS as your LORD and SAVIOUR from sin and it's consequences – separation from GOD and judgement

Dear LORD JESUS,

I believe that you died on the cross for me. I believe that you died in my place for all my sins, all that I have done wrong. I thank You that You loved me enough to give Your life as a sacrifice for mine. I receive your love for me right now; I ask that you take away my sins and all that has been wrong in my life. Please wash me clean and come to live in my heart. I accept you as my LORD and Saviour. Thank you for saving me, for coming into my heart and life. I love you and receive the eternal life that You give right now. Thank You LORD JESUS! Amen.

A prayer to receive the baptism of The HOLY SPIRIT and His gifts

Dear FATHER-GOD,

I thank you for sending JESUS I have received as my LORD and Saviour. Thank You that I now qualify for Your promise to also me to be filled with the power of The HOLY SPIRIT. I come to You on the basis of Your Word, the Bible and right now ask You to fill me, drench me and flood me to overflowing with Your precious gift of the HOLY SPIRIT. HOLY SPIRIT I receive You into my life now in a unique, personal, powerful and special way. Thank You as You fill me, for the gifts You also have to give me especially the divine ability to speak in other tongues and prophecy. I ask for and believe You for these gifts to show up in my life right away! Thank You my FATHER! Thank You LORD JESUS! Thank You precious and dear HOLY SPIRIT! Amen.

Published   by   SERVANT   MINISTRIES

Other books by the same author

1. **LEST WE FORGET** – The life and times of the pioneer missionaries to Ibadan, Nigeria (1851 – 1868) As a young girl Anna's dream was to one day be a martyr for JESUS. This is the powerful story of her life along with her husband David, who were the first Christian missionaries to Ibadan in southwest Nigeria from 1851 to 1868. As you read it you will be impacted by a life on fire for GOD!

2. **THE WELLS OF OUR FATHERS** - A history of revival in southwest Nigeria from 1830 to 1959. But this is far more than a history lesson, this is about honouring the lives of all who have gone before us and laid foundations. It is on these foundations that we stand and ascend to the next levels of faith and reformation that The HOLY SPIRIT has in store for us. Life and grace are released as we honour these generals, prophets and apostles who have preceded us. We owe them.

3. **TRANSITION** – Something new is on the horizon! Highlighting areas that The HOLY SPIRIT is revealing to His saints where emphasis and change are needed to break old moulds and be supple to be able to contain the new wine falling on the church. This book starts off with a list of 25 such areas then hones in on six of them including restoration of the prophetic and apostolic offices.

4. **CROSSOVER!** – A manual for transcending societal & cultural obstacles for maximum impact. This book is a reminder of the love The FATHER has for the cultures and nations of the world. Featuring practical ways for social contextulisation including how to conduct socially open church services and contemporary evangelistic paradigms. The FATHER's love is portrayed for us as individuals freeing us to our unique and precious identities.

5. **YOU CAN PROPHESY! 70 truths about the gift of prophecy** - A handy and concise resource covering 22 Reasons to Prophesy, 7 Ways to Prepare for Prophetic Words and Encounters, 7 Ways to Activate Prophetic Grace and loads more. This book presents prophesy as a gift available to every believer, it is not a mark of some great level or height of spirituality.

6. **TRAINING & ACTIVATION MANUALS** – *Equipping the saints (Ephesians 4:11)* - Three resources for training in all righteousness that the man of GOD may be fully equipped in primary areas of the faith. – *Equipping the saints (Ephesians 4:11)*

   a. **25 types of Prayer, Tongues and Interpretation** – all in one manual. LORD teach us to pray was the cry of the disciples, 'LORD make it ours too!'

   b. **Prophecy and Prophetic evangelism** – this gift belongs to us! It is not just

111

for the super saint! Covering all the basics you need to walk in prophecy as your spiritual inheritance.

c. **Faith, Working Of Miracles & Gifts Of Healings – 21 ways GOD heals today!**

Printed in Great Britain
by Amazon